GIRL TALK

10 Life-Changing Conversations about Biblical Womanhood

*A topical Bible Study by
Margy Hill*

Introduction

"From time to time talk becomes effective, conquering like war, widening the boundaries of knowledge like an exploration."

Robert Louis Stevenson

The definition of a conversation is a *sharing* of thoughts and ideas. One online dictionary uses the example of two friends talking while having coffee together. I love coffee and conversation, especially when it is centered on the Word of God. Seldom do we take the time to gather together as women and "talk" our way through the Scriptures. The kind of "talks" where we ask the hard questions, engage one another in life-changing conversations, exposing the lies of the culture in an effort to bring biblical truth to the forefront. It is precisely this type of conversation that promotes a deeper walk with God and authenticity with His people.

"Girl Talk" is a series of conversations challenging women to embrace their *womanhood, biblical womanhood*. You may not have noticed, but the truths of biblical womanhood are under attack, being challenged both by the culture and the church. Every woman, whether she recognizes it or not, has been influenced by "feminist" thinking. She takes these thoughts with her into her home, her workplace, her ministry and out into the world, not understanding that her ideas have consequences. In order to be a light to the world around her, a woman must know what it is that she believes, so that she can fulfill her Titus role, and influence the generation coming up after her.

It's not difficult today to find books on the topic of biblical womanhood, but each author brings with their writing a personal opinion, a "bent" that leaves the reader with a "little bit of the Bible" and a lot of the writer's influential thought. It is not enough to embrace what other writers believe about biblical womanhood; we must come to the One who is the expert on the topic.

Author Mary Kassian in her book, "The Feminist Mistake", prays that "… God will raise up holy "Issachar" men and women to speak to the next generation – men and women who hold the knowledge of our times in one hand and the Word of God in the other, men and women whose hearts are broken over the gender confusion and spiritual/emotional carnage of our day and who (like those men of old) know what the church should do (1 Chronicles 12:32)."[i]

"Girl Talk" is my contribution to restore the truth of biblical womanhood. I pray that as you dig deep into the Scriptures, you will discover truth for yourself, and join me in my efforts. May we believe, embrace and teach the next generation, what it means to be a woman. In this, God receives all the glory He deserves and women are able to truly live the abundant life!

Though it's not possible for me to sit down with every one of you over coffee and enjoy the conversation, know that I am praying for you!

Helpful Guidelines

My husband currently serves as the Small Groups pastor at our church. The two of us have been heavily involved in small group ministry for seventeen years. We have witnessed time and time again the power of authentic community to form strong Christian relationships and create devoted and committed followers of Jesus Christ. This takes place as the Scriptures are expounded and applied to everyday life.

Girl Talk is unique as a Bible study in that it is designed to promote deep discussion and transforming conversation among women. Be encouraged that the "path" has already been traveled on. As with all of my Bible studies, I have already taken a small group of women through Girl Talk. I was surprised to see, not only how quickly the women began to talk, but how honest and transparent they were in sharing.

My suggestion for the women's ministry leader, as she takes her women through Girl Talk, is to incorporate a 20 minute teaching on the topic presented, allowing the remaining time in the evening for small groups. Be creative with this 20 minutes using media (videos, skits, current events, etc.) to peak interest. Keep your groups smaller in size so that your women will feel at ease in participating in the conversation. Be sure that your leaders are prepared to facilitate the discussion, and resist the temptation to teach. The questions are written to engage women in biblical truths and an open discussion will help them to work through what it is they truly believe. At the end of the evening, allow time for a representative from each group to share one truth they gleaned from their time of conversation. This is important in bringing the women to together to celebrate what they have learned.

Last, but certainly not least, all matters are settled by the Word of God. The Word of God is the "final" word! Bibles should be open at all times and its pages should be continually turning! This will prevent personal opinion from ruling the discussion.

I want to thank you for your participation in "Girl Talk." In your efforts to help your women understand and live out the truths of biblical womanhood, you are walking in the obedience of Titus 2:3-5. You are also supporting the efforts to revive the glorious truths of womanhood in a day where they are being considered, "outdated." Please know I am available to answer any questions that you might have and to offer suggestions for bringing "Girl Talk" to your church. If you would like to kick off the study with a "Girl Talk" seminar, I would love to come and encourage your women.

Love in Christ,

Margy Hill

E-mail: mhill@wmconnection.org or leroyandmargyhill@gmail.com

A Woman's Identity and Role

Conversation 1   Equal or Unequal?

Conversation 2   Feminism or Femininity?

Conversation 3   Helper or 2nd Class Assignment?

Conversation 4   Lifegiver or Taker?

Conversation 5   A House or a Home?

A Woman's Character

Conversation 6   To Submit or Not Submit?

Conversation 7   Daring or Discrete?

Conversation 8   Meekness or Weakness?

Conversation 9   Women or Men?

Conversation 10   Retire or Inspire?

EQUAL OR UNEQUAL?

So God created man in His own image; in the image of God He created him; male and female He created them.

Genesis 1:27

The Conversation

Genesis 1:27 is clear to teach that God created both male and female in His image. As His creation, men and women were created equally, sharing the same value, worth and significance. Wayne Grudem aptly describes this equality:

If men and women are equal in the image of God, then we are equally important to God and equally valuable to Him. We have equal worth before Him for all eternity, for this is how we were created. This truth should exclude all our feelings of pride or inferiority and should exclude any idea that one sex is "better" or "worse" than the other. In contrast to many non-Christian cultures and religions, no one should feel proud or superior because he is a man, and no one should feel disappointed or inferior because she is a woman. If God thinks us to be equal in value, then that settles forever the question of personal worth, for God's evaluation is the true standard.[ii]

This 1st conversation is critical. We must know and understand that God does not see women as inferior nor does His Word condone or teach it.

Let's Talk…

1. What do the following verses declare about your worth and value in God's estimation?

    - Psalm 139:13-16

    - John 1:12

    - Romans 8:17

- 2 Corinthians 6:18

- Ephesians 2:10

- 1 John 3:1

2. Why is it so important that a woman understand and live in the truth of her worth, value and significance in Christ?

3. Explain Paul's statement in Galatians 3:28?

4. We see additional evidence of a man and woman's equality in the image of God in the New Testament church. What do you discover from the following verses?

 - Acts 2:17-18

 - Acts 2:41

- 1 Corinthians 12:7, 11

- 1 Peter 4:10

5. Read Acts 10:34 in the King James Version: *Then Peter opened his mouth, and said, of a truth I perceive that God is no respecter of persons…*

What does Peter mean by, "God is no respecter of persons?"

6. Ponder this additional insight by Caleb Colley Ph.D. with Apologetics Press:

God offers salvation to every man, no matter what external circumstances, such as socioeconomic status or nationality, might apply to him. God does not offer salvation only to the Jew, just because he is a Jew, or only to the Gentile because he is a Gentile. The Greek word translated "respecter of persons" in the King James Version of Acts 10:34 ("God is no respecter of persons") is **prosopolemptes**, *a word that refers to a judge who looks at a man's face instead of at the facts of the case, and makes a decision based on whether or not he likes the man (Lenski, 1961, p. 418). Under Roman law, for example, a defendant's societal status was weighed heavily along with evidence. Any human judge might show undue favor to a plaintiff or a defendant because of private friendship, bribery, rank, power, or political affiliation, but God, the perfect Judge, cannot be tempted by any of the things that might tempt a human judge to show unfair partiality.*[iii]

Look up the following verses and indicate how they support the truth of God's impartiality.

- 2 Chronicles 19:7

- Job 34:19

- John 3:16

- Romans 2:10-11

- 1 Peter 1:17

- 2 Peter 3:9

7. Read James 2:1-4 in the New Living Translation.

My dear brothers and sisters, how can you claim to have faith in our glorious Lord Jesus Christ if you favor some people over others? For example, suppose someone comes into your meeting dressed in fancy clothes and expensive jewelry, and another comes in who is poor and dressed in dirty clothes. If you give special attention and a good seat to the rich person, but you say to the poor one, "You can stand over there, or else sit on the floor"—well, doesn't this discrimination show that your judgments are guided by evil motives?

Look up the word "discrimination" in a dictionary. Have you ever been tempted to think that God and His word is discriminatory? Explain your answer.

8. Based on James 2:1-4 who is responsible for the sin of discrimination?

9. Take a moment to draw some conclusions about "inequality".

   The last decades have seen the rise of a society that is so concerned with political correctness and so sensitive to being "offended" that civility has lost its way. However, this is really nothing new, for there has always been inequality in the world. It is sad but true that artificial barriers have always divided humanity—barriers that have no basis in God's Word. It is sin in the heart that causes inequality. It is sin that causes men to treat women in ways that are meant to demean or objectify them. And it is sin that seeks counterfeit solutions to counteract these inequalities. The only true cure for inequality is obedience to God's Word. If men and women would walk in obedience to God's Word, radical feminism would be seen for what it is, and the harmony that God has ordained between men and women would result.[iv]

   S. Michael Houdmann

   Would you agree or disagree that obedience to God's Word is the true remedy for inequality? Why or why not?

10. Scripture teaches that inequality is due to the sinful heart of men but inequality is not the heart of God. Now that you have had an opportunity to consider what the Bible teaches, do you believe that women are created unequally or equally to men? Why or why not?

FEMINISM OR FEMININITY?

*And the Lord God caused a deep sleep to fall on Adam, and he slept; and He took one of his ribs, and closed up the flesh in its place. Then the rib which the Lord God had taken from man He made into a **woman**, and He brought her to the man.*

Genesis 2:21-22

The Conversation

Though the words *feminism* and *femininity* appear to be similar, they are very different in their definition. *Feminism* pertains to the advocacy of women's rights on the grounds of political, social, and economic equality. *Femininity,* on the other hand, is the quality of being female. It is also called womanliness or womanhood. *Femininity* is a set of attributes, behaviors and roles generally associated with girls and women.

> *According to Elisabeth Elliot, "That word 'femininity' is one that we don't hear very often anymore. We've heard the word 'feminist' quite often in the last couple of decades, but we haven't really heard much about the deep mystery that is called femininity. Holding to a biblical view of femininity is quite unpopular in our contemporary society; it is frequently perceived as demeaning, inferior, and limiting. Regrettably, this attitude has now affected American evangelicalism so that the issue must be clarified by recovering a biblical worldview of femininity.*[v]

In the book, "Becoming God's True Woman", contributing author Carolyn Mahaney further discusses femininity:

When God created the first woman, He made a fully feminine creature. You and I did not become feminine because someone gave us a doll and put a dress on us—we were born feminine because we were created feminine. The feminist doctrine of our time upholds the notion that femininity is a matter of cultural conditioning. Many feminists argue that the only essential difference between men and women is our anatomy, but Genesis teaches otherwise. Because God created male and female, we women are innately feminine. Granted, a woman can accentuate her femininity or she can detract from it, but she cannot change it— our sex chromosomes are in every cell of our bodies. Our femininity is a gift of grace from a loving God.[vi]

Christian women are to define womanhood based on the timeless truths found in the Word of God. This conversation will provide a deeper understanding of "biblical womanhood" and help us to differentiate between the lies of cultural feminism and the truth of biblical femininity.

Let's Talk...

1. "Feminist theology" began when women viewed their role as not equal to men. We shouldn't be surprised, the battle of the sexes began long ago in the garden. Consider the truth of Genesis 3:16 (b) in the NLT... ***And you will desire to control your husband, but he will rule over you.***

    - Based on this verse, what do you learn about the sinful nature of men and women?

2. The definition of "femininity" or "womanhood" is a set of attributes, behaviors and roles, generally associated with girls and women. Using Scripture to support your answer, provide an example of two or three of these attributes, behaviors or roles.

3. As you consider the different definitions presented in this conversation, what problems might arise between what God teaches us about femininity versus what the culture teaches us about feminism?

4. Mary Kassian in her book, "The Feminist Mistake" the progression of the Feminist movement. First woman demanded the right to define herself, then she demanded the right to define the world around her and finally she demanded the right to define God.

Feminism began with the deconstruction of a Judeo-Christian view of womanhood (the right to name self; 1960-1970); progressed to the deconstruction of manhood, gender relationships, family/societal structures, and a Judeo-Christian worldview (the right to name the world; 1970-1980); and concluded with the concept of metaphysical pluralism, self-deification, and the rejection of the Judeo-Christian deity (the right to name God; 1980-1990).[vii]

Share your understanding of the feminist movement throughout the years. How has the movement impacted your life?

5. Feminism is a philosophy that advocates equal rights for women and men—socially, politically, economically, and in other ways. In its early stages, we see fairness demanded for a women's right to vote and equal work opportunities and wages. However, today we see a feminism that seeks to neutralize gender, defend abortion on demand and promote lesbianism. Radical feminists deny any difference between men and women, teaching that any perceived differences between the sexes are due solely to social conditioning. Modern feminism is a counterfeit solution to the real issue of the inequality of women in a sinful society. Feminism arrogates to itself the right to demand respect and equality in every aspect of life. Feminism is based in arrogance, and it is the opposite of the call to the born-again believer to be a servant. The modern, militant feminists call women to rise up and rebel against the order that God has given to mankind. That brand of feminism seeks to impose humanistic values in direct opposition to the Word of God. Feminism was originally a positive movement, focused on giving women the basic rights God intends for every human being to have. Tragically, feminism now focuses on destroying all distinctions in the roles of men and women.[viii]

S. Michael Houdmann

- Do you agree with the author's assessment of feminism? Explain your answer.

6. What strong warning does Colossians 2:8 issue to believers?

7. Identify some of the world's philosophies about women.

8. Do you think that some of these "problems" have found their way into the Church? Why or why not?

9. Make a list identifying some of the lies from the culture you have believed about womanhood that have caused you to suffer greatly.

10. Women believe that feminism will bring them the freedom and power they deserve. Is there anything questionable that you find in that line of thinking? Share your thoughts.

HELPER OR 2ND CLASS ASSIGNMENT?

And the Lord God said, "It is not good that man should be alone; I will make him a helper comparable to him."

Genesis 2:18

The Conversation

Men and women both bear the image of God; yet they have different roles, and different expressions that allow them to glorify God in very distinct ways. Despite this biblical truth, a debate continues in the church. There are those who believe that anyone, male or female, should be allowed to assume any position in the Church (egalitarians) and those who believe that while men and women are equal, God has assigned them different roles (complementarians). Scripture is clear to teach a "complementarian" view.

The Hebrew word "ezer" or "helper" is a "beautiful" word and is often used throughout Scripture to describe God. Unfortunately, the culture with its' feminist bias has assigned its own definition of helper to mean "subservient." Consider Criswell's insight:

The woman is the perfect counterpart of man, possessing neither inferiority nor superiority, but being like and equal in personhood, and unique and different in function. Genesis 2:18 emphasizes man's need for a companion, a helper, and an equal. He was incomplete without someone to complement him in fulfilling the task of filling, multiplying, and taking dominion over the earth. This points to Adam's inadequacy, not Eve's insufficiency. Woman was made by God to meet man's deficiency.[ix]

WA Criswell

The New Bible Commentary explains the companionship of marriage:

The husband and wife complement each other. Suitable helper would be better-translated 'helper matching him', i.e. supplying what he lacks. She is his missing rib. Matthew Henry commented on God's choice of a rib to create Eve: 'Not made out of his head to top him, not out of his feet to be trampled upon by him, but out of his side to be equal with him, under his arm to be protected, and near his heart to be loved.' Perhaps this reads a little too much into the rib, but it expresses well the biblical ideal of marriage.[x]

A helper role is a *completer* role. A women's help brings a great influence to the home, the workplace, the community, the church and the world at large. This role applies to a woman whether she is married or not. Women do not need to usurp the leadership role of men; they are there to complement it and help to complete it.

It is a distinctive calling of God to display the glory of His Son in ways that would not be displayed if there were no womanhood. If there were only generic persons and not male and female, the glory of Christ would be diminished in the world. When God described the glorious work of His Son as the sacrifice of a husband for his bride, He was telling us why He made us male and female. He made us this way so that our maleness and femaleness would display more fully the glory of his Son in relation to His blood-bought bride.[xi]

John Piper

Let's Talk...

1. What are some reasons that a woman might consider her role as "helper" as a second class assignment?

2. Who does the word "helper" refer to in Psalm 121? Describe how this "Helper" assists us according to this psalm.

3. Considering your answer to the previous question, would you agree that the word "helper" does not imply inferiority? Why or why not?

4. What additional information do we learn about the role of "helper" from the following verses?

    - 1 Samuel 7:12

    - Psalm 10:14

- Psalm 28:7

- Psalm 54:4

- Psalm 72:12

- Psalm 86:17

5. From these verses we see God as our Helper, who comes to our rescue, who comforts us in times of trouble and is merciful toward us. In His role as Helper, we clearly see the attribute of His compassion manifested in His loving and protective relationship with His people.

    Share some ways you have experienced a desire to extend compassion to those in need. Did it ever occur to you that those desires were placed in your heart by God and that in that role you glorify God in your womanhood? Why or why not?

6. How do women bring a deeper sense of community and compassion into the Body of Christ?

7. List the ways that you see the wife supporting her husband in Proverbs 31:10-31.

8. If you are married, write down in your own words what it means to be a "helper."

9. If you are single, provide some ways you can be motivated by your understanding of the word "helper" to infuse compassion into your sphere of influence.

10. Rather than resenting our calling as helpers, we should rejoice in this side of our feminine design. In what ways have you been most impacted as you consider your role of helper?

LIFEGIVER OR TAKER?

And Adam called his wife's name Eve, because she was the mother of all living. Genesis 3:20

The Conversation

As women, though we bear the results of Eve's sin, we also bear her name. From Genesis 2:18 through Genesis 3:19, Eve is known as "woman" but in verse 20, Adam names Eve. Eve's name in the Hebrew means "life" or "life-giving," or "mother of all who have life." Have you ever wondered what Adam might have been thinking as he pondered a name for Eve? Authors Donald Davidson and Sally Clarkson both offer interesting insights:

"In view of the awful judgment pronounced upon them, the man might have been pardoned if he had reproached her as 'death,' for it was her sin that brought death into our world and all our woe. But Adam gives her a name which is expressive of the prophetic life bound up in her. For through the seed of the woman, sin would one day be vanquished, and death would be swallowed up in victory."[xii]

Donald Davidson - Mothers in the Bible

The Hebrew word for Eve (*chavah*) expresses both the essence of life itself and the creative ability to grant that life to others. Imagine the command to be fruitful and multiply without women! Perhaps for a woman there is no more beautiful role than that of a life-giver. And we do ourselves a grave injustice if we limit that role to only physical childbirth.

"Not every woman will marry. Not every woman will be able to bear children. And yet all women have the God-given capacity to live in ways that beautifully and purposefully express their life-giving feminine design -their helper or cooperative approach to tasks, their ability to multitask, their nesting instincts and creative spirit. A woman's body was made, in part, to bring life into the world, and that's a good thing from God's point of view. However, the common purpose for all woman is to glorify God in whatever circumstances and boundaries of life we find ourselves, trusting Him to show us how we can best use our gifts for Him.[xiii]

Sally Clarkson – Mission Motherhood

Orientation to mother is given by God to women, our desire to nurture, to nourish, to support and encourage. The nurturing aspects of women display the glory of El Shaddai! El Shaddai means God Almighty. "El" pointing to the power of God Himself, but "Shaddai" seems to be derived from another word meaning "breast", which implies that Shaddai signifies the One who nourishes, supplies, and satisfies. We immediately think of God who designed a woman's breasts to give life and support to her newborn. It is God as "El" who helps, but it is God as "Shaddai" who abundantly blesses. As life-giving women, we bring glory to God when we nurture and nourish those around us.

Let's Talk...

1. Look up the word "nurture" and write out the definition. Describe some ways that women demonstrate their "nurturing."

2. Read and write out Isaiah 66:13.

3. Consider Spurgeon's comments on God's choice to compare His comfort to that of a mother:

   This is a peculiarly delightful metaphor. A father can comfort, but I think he is not much at home in the work. When God speaks about His pity, He compares Himself to the father. "Like as a father pities his children, so the Lord pities them that fear Him." But when He speaks about comfort, He selects the mother. When I have seen the little ones sick, I have felt all the pity in the world for them, but I did not know how to set to work to comfort them—but a mother knows by instinct how to do it! There is placed in the mother's tender heart a power of sympathy and very soon she finds the word or gives the touch that will meet her darling's case and cheer its troubled soul.[xiv]

   Do you think that God was purposeful in using the illustration of a mother's comfort to highlight an aspect of biblical womanhood? Explain your answer.

4. It is important to note that "mothering" is not only possible in the "physical" but also the spiritual. Beth Moore comments, *"God created every life to be fruitful and multiply, but this God-given dream represents more than physical offspring. I believe our dreams to have babies represent a desire to have fruitful lives, to invest ourselves in something that matters and makes a difference."*[xv]

In what ways is spiritual mothering applicable to "all women?" Use Scripture to support your answer.

5. Tammy Maltby, in her book "Lifegiving", defines lifegiving as God's fingerprint on the heart of women. *"It's who God created us to be," she continues, reminding us that all our acts of love and service, the daily offerings of lifegiving, are seen by our unseen God. Women who are committed to developing and expressing the lifegiving aspect of their natures embrace the value of their drive to nurture and nourish life around them. They are compassionate, caring, thoughtful and creative. In Genesis 3:20, Adam changed Woman's name to Eve because she was to become the mother of all living things. Life givers is who we are whether or not we ever have children. We not only give physical life, but spiritual life, intellectual life and cultural life. The holidays we plan, the music we play, the candles we light, the scrapbooks we keep, the meals we prepare, the words we say all give life."*[xvi]

Based on Tammy's comments, share some ways that you have been a life-giver.

6. Unfortunately we live in a culture whose motto is live this life for **YOU**! The world holds a mindset completely contrary to Scripture, encouraging women to *take* life instead of *give* it. Children are thought of as a hindrance and not a blessing.

Provide some examples that reveal the heart of the culture towards children.

7. How does Psalm 127:3 stand in opposition to the world's view on children?

8. In a culture like ours, where it is so easy to have an abortion, we have to keep God's truth in the forefront of our mind. *Children are a heritage, they are a reward.* They belong to God, are entrusted to our care, and are indicative of His blessing. Abortion serves to murder an unwanted child and to take an innocent life in the womb.

    What does God ask of believers in Psalm 24:11-12 and what are some practical ways we can walk in obedience to this command?

    An Important Note: *You may be a woman who suffered an abortion. Remember that the blood of Christ has covered your sin and there is grace for you. Many of you have found healing and made the decision to serve in local pregnancy centers to save the lives of the unborn and to share your testimony and the good news of Jesus Christ. You are a life-giver! If you have not yet received God's comfort and healing for your abortion, take time to invest in a post-abortive Bible study offered at your local pregnancy center.*

9. There are a web of lies wrapped within the statement, "a woman has the right to choose." This idea suggests that a woman's body belongs to her and she can do with it as she pleases. What is the truth of Scripture revealed in in 1 Corinthians 6:19-20?

10. There is a sense in which the Christian has no "rights" of her own, because she has surrendered her life to Christ. Is it possible for a Christian woman to be pro-choice? Why or why not?

A HOUSE OR A HOME?

The wise woman builds her house, but the foolish pulls it down with her hands. Proverbs 14:1

The Conversation

Back in the sixties, Burt Bacharach wrote a song called, "A House is Not a Home".[xvii] The lyrics describe a house without people in it, a house empty of relationship. Today many houses are not homes that enjoy the presence of wise women building them.

We quickly see in the Book of Genesis, that Satan declared war on what God called good in Genesis 1:31. He tempted Eve to doubt the goodness and love of her Creator. She reached for what was forbidden and sin entered the world. Eve was deceived and instead of believing in the awesome plan that God had for her life, she fell for the lie. The crux of Satan's lie will always be that God is not good and either is His plan. Satan says there is something better.

What are the lies in the culture today that come against a woman being a home builder? There are many, but let's look at five that have served Satan well.

- Gender Neutrality. *There are no differences between men and women.*
- Equality. *To be equal, men and women must be the same.*
- A Career. *The home is not a place worthy of our best labors.*
- Children. *They are not a blessing, but a hindrance.*
- Two Incomes. *A higher standard of living is more important than the family.*

God sent His Son, Jesus, to defeat these lies and to give us the abundant life. His design for women to be homebuilders glorifies Him in ways that His roles for men never could. When we walk outside of His beautiful design, we are being robbed and cheated of all that God has for us as women.

Instead of embracing our role in the home, Satan has us chasing after the things of the world that leave us tired and disappointed. I am one of those women who fell for the lie before I came to Christ. The lie ended two marriages and the struggle of living life as a single mom took me down the thief's path – first to steal, then kill and finally destroy. I am so thankful that Christ saved me and opened my eyes to the truth. Now I have a heart to help women, married or single, walk in the joy of God's intended design for their life.

Home economic courses that I remember taking in high school are now obsolete, being replaced by units on personal finance, career development, and how to be a responsible consumer. Domestic training for girls is unheard of. Now we understand why the role of a Titus woman is so critical in the church today. It is our responsibility as Christian women to provide the teaching and training of our young women and to help them make their house a home.

We are tempted to believe that the work of a home builder is inferior to other opportunities. But we need to see our homes as a ministry, a real mission field where lives are changed by our eternal investment. Our homes are our mission fields, a high and holy calling. If we are missing in action, there is no one to take our place and the home falls apart. Someone once said of Edith Schaeffer, *"As many people were brought to the Lord through Mrs. Schaeffer's cinnamon buns as through Dr. Schaeffer's sermons."*[xviii] It's something to think about.

Let's Talk...

By no means is this week's study designed to attack or condemn the working woman. It is intended to reach the woman who has believed the lie that being a wife and mother is not valuable and is convinced that a career is her way to personal fulfillment. Also, single women please know you play an equally important role in this discussion.

1. Read Acts 16:11-15. What do you learn about Lydia?

2. Lydia not only opened up her heart to Jesus, but also her home. There is no mention in Scripture that Lydia was married, but she was the mistress of her own household. The other members of her household probably included some family members as well as slaves that worked in her business. Lydia opened up her home and the first church plant in Europe was born!

    Would Lydia fit the description of Romans 12:13? Why or why not?

3. Define "hospitality". In what ways do you see women excel in the area of hospitality?

4. Lydia is a beautiful example of hospitality. Often we miss the "depth" of meaning in the word, "hospitality" and think of it as simply "entertaining". That may be the cultural idea but consider this insight:

The word hospitality is a kin of hospital.[xix] Now we rarely put those two words together in our culture because the mental images they generate are so different. But a hospital is a place away from your home that is designed to bring healing and wholeness. Hospitality is not about a vacation, but about allowing your home and your presence to bring emotional, mental, and spiritual healing to others.

J.D. Davis
Lydia: A Model of Service and Hospitality - Acts 16

In his book *Outlive Your Life*, Max Lucado writes:

"Long before the church had pulpits and baptisteries, she had kitchens and dinner tables. Even a casual reading of the New Testament unveils the house as the primary tool of the church. The primary gathering place of the church was the home. The early church (with its varied backgrounds got along) without the aid of sanctuaries, church buildings, clergy, or seminaries. They did so through the clearest of messages (the Cross) and the simplest of tools (the home).

Something holy happens around a dinner table that will never happen in a sanctuary. In a church auditorium you see the backs of heads. Around the table you see the expressions on faces. Church services are on the clock. Around the table there is time to talk. When you open your door to someone, you are sending this message: 'You matter to me and to God.' You may think you are saying, 'Come over for a visit.' But what your guest hears is, 'I am worth the effort.'"[xx]

Do you find the role of homebuilder and hospitality significant in God's eternal plan? Why or why not?

5. What are some of the reasons women have frowned upon this role?

6. Again consider Tammy Maltby's insight:

   The issue today is whether women today in the process of pursuing respect in the career world have lost something in their identity as women. Who is making "homemade" anything today? Who is bringing fresh flowers, lighting candles for the family to enjoy, thinking about the extra touches, the seemingly insignificant lifegiving activities that nurture and nourish, that create warmth and security at home and in society?[xxi]

   Whether you are married or single, what are some practical ways that you can make your "house" a "home"?

7. It was women who gave the early church the warmth and the hospitality that allowed it to flourish. Romans 16 is filled with the names of women who worked hard for the gospel, who believed that their mission station was their home. Pick one of the women from Romans 16 and describe their legacy.

8. It is not an exaggeration to claim that many women today find themselves trying to maintain a job, family, household and ministry. We are often stressed, exhausted, drained and overcommitted. It's time to re-evaluate our lives because it is not the life that God has called us to live. We are to live out our roles in the way God planned.

   Read Proverbs 31:30. It's important to note that the Proverbs 31 woman had many responsibilities too, but what does this verse reveal about her priority?

9. "Fear" in the context of Proverbs 31:30 "does not mean that we must live in constant dread and worry of God's punishment. Instead the fear of the Lord is loving reverence of God that includes submission to His Lordship and to the commands of His Word (NIV Study Bible)."

   Why is our relationship with God and His Word *vital* as we seek to be women who are homebuilders?

10. Would you agree that the times when your life is most "out of control" is often when you have spent the least time with God? What are some ways you can reverse that trend?

TO SUBMIT OR NOT SUBMIT?

Submitting to one another in the fear of God.

Ephesians 5:21

The Conversation

To submit or not submit, that is the question! Not only the question, but the struggle. Why is the word "submission" so threatening for women? Earlier in the study we covered Genesis 3:16 and learned that our default (fleshly) desire is to control and rule.

In a perfect world, before sin, Adam deeply loved Eve. With complete trust in that love, she came under and yielded to his leadership. But sin spoiled God's design for marriage. The man who was to lovingly care for and nurture his wife would now seek to rule her, and the wife would desire to take control from her husband. Understanding our flesh and the natural desire we have to take authority from our husbands is the first key to understanding submission. We now know our struggle is no longer imagined, but real! Submission is impossible in our flesh!

We also struggle in this area if we limit our understanding of submission to marriage only. It is important that we take a deeper look at the word and open up the fullness of its definition.

The Greek word for "submission" is "hupotasso", a Greek military term meaning "to arrange [troop divisions] in a military fashion under the command of a leader". In its non-military use it was a "voluntary attitude of giving in, cooperating, assuming responsibility, and carrying a burden". (New Testament Greek Lexicon)

What we need to embrace about this definition is that submission is an "attitude" of the heart, an attitude that is cooperative and yielded to placing oneself under another. This attitude is beautifully pictured for us as we look at the example of Christ in Philippians 2:1-8:

Is there any such thing as Christians cheering each other up? Do you love me enough to want to help me? Does it mean anything to you that we are brothers in the Lord, sharing the same Spirit? Are your hearts tender and sympathetic at all? Then make me truly happy by loving each other and agreeing wholeheartedly with each other, working together with one heart and mind and purpose. Don't be selfish; don't live to make a good impression on others. Be humble, thinking of others as better than yourself. Don't just think about your own affairs, but be interested in others, too, and in what they are doing. Your attitude should be the kind that was shown us by Jesus Christ, who, though he was God, did not demand and cling to his rights as God, but laid aside his mighty power and glory, taking the disguise of a slave and becoming like men. And he humbled himself even further, going so far as actually to die a criminal's death on a cross. (The Living Bible)

We are to willingly place ourselves under Christ, under our churches, under one another, under our husbands, under our employers, and under our government with the same attitude that was shown to us by Jesus Christ, an attitude of humility. This Christ-like attitude is a kingdom attitude, designed for us to enjoy healthy relationships with one another and to glorify God in the unbelieving world we live in. Broadening our scope and understanding of submission will help us to walk it out in every relationship.

Let's Talk...

1. Share your personal struggle with submission whether it exists in marriage, the workplace, other relationships or the government.

2. Perhaps the biggest misunderstanding of submission is explained well by Dr. Wayne Grudem.

   Submission to authority can be totally consistent with equality in importance, dignity, and honor. Jesus was subject to both His parents and to God the Father but was not lower than either of them. Thus the command to wives to be subject to their husbands should never be taken to imply inferior personhood or spirituality, or lesser importance.

   Based on the above comment, what have you believed about biblical submission?

3. Submission is a kingdom principle based on Christ's model of servanthood. Record the dispute between the disciples in Mark 9:33-35. Give some practical examples of "wanting to be first" or "the greatest" from everyday life.

4. Jesus dealt with the disciple's pride. A prideful attitude is easy to spot; it is selfish, haughty, impatient and controlling. The prideful heart rebels against authority and wants its own way no matter the cost.

    In contrast, what does the attitude of humility look like? Use Scripture to support your answer.

5. Read and write out Proverbs 29:23. What does it mean when the author writes "a man's pride will bring him low?"

6. Now that we have a better understanding of what submission is, let's take a closer look and see how submission is to practically play out in our lives. Though Sarah, the wife of Abraham, offers us a great and commonly used biblical example, we will look at Abigail, who also is one of those women Peter describes in 1 Peter 3:5: *For in this manner, in former times, the holy women who trusted in God also adorned themselves, being submissive to their own husbands.*

    Read 1 Samuel 25:2-43. Contrast the description of Abigail to Nabal in 1 Samuel 25:3.

7. What additional information do you learn about Nabal's character in these verses?

- 1 Samuel 25:11

- 1 Samuel 25:17

- 1 Samuel 25:25

- 1 Samuel 25:36

8. Abigail found herself in the middle of a trying circumstance completely brought about by her husband. Describe what some of her responses might have been had she reacted "in her flesh".

9. Abigail acted in wisdom. We see a very wise woman seek to risk her life to spare her husband's and those men in her household. Abigail chose to place her husband's life above her own and intercede before David on Nabal's behalf. This is true submission and we learn a valuable lesson – submission is not always expressed in obedience to men. Abigail submitted first to God and the Word of God.

The Hebrew word "sekel" is used to describe Abigail's character. "Sekel" implies that she was a woman of prudence, discretion and good sense. Look up the definition of "prudent" to gain a better understanding of this aspect of Abigail's character. What does Scripture teach about this quality?

- Proverbs 8:12

- Proverbs 13:16

- Proverbs 14:15

- Proverbs 15:5

- Proverbs 19:14

10. What important truths do we learn about submission from Abigail and examples like her in the Bible?

    - Shiprah and Puah: Exodus 1:15-20

    - Shadrach, Meshach and Abednego: Daniel 3:12-18

    - The disciples: Acts 5:22-29

Conclude by writing a paragraph summarizing the truths you have learned about "an attitude of submission". What do you need to do to begin to develop this attitude in your life?

DARING OR DISCREET

As a ring of gold in a swine's snout, so is a lovely woman who lacks discretion. Proverbs 11:22

The Conversation

Webster's Collegiate Dictionary says that discretion is the quality of being discreet; cautious; reserved in speech; with the ability to make responsible decisions. The biblical definition defines the word as "taste" and "judgment".

If you were to ask a young woman today, what it means to be discreet, you would quickly discover she may have never heard the word before. I believe that is because discretion and its value as a virtue in a woman's life is being lost to the culture. In a world of social media where women dare to take what should be private and make it public, we shouldn't be surprised when indiscretion rears its ugly head.

Can you picture a pig with a beautiful gold ring through its nose? The beauty of the ring is in no way becoming to the pig. Now imagine a beautiful woman who has no self-control. Her conduct in no way reflects the woman God intended her to be. To compare the character of an Israelite woman to that of a pig was an extreme insult, but it communicates a far more valuable lesson that women today need to embrace.

In an attempt at gaining attention, some women feel the need to be seen. This insecurity drives them to often flaunt their outward appearance by dressing in a less than modest way. Their lack of self-control causes them to give way to their feelings and emotions, leading to rash and often unwise decisions. Perhaps the best example is a woman who is thoughtless in her speech, talking about anything and everything without any filter or consideration of others in her comments. One writer beautifully describes God's original design:

God has called Christian women to stand out from the women of the world. They are to be an example of how God created a woman to be. A Christian woman with discretion does not need to be the center of attention. Instead, she finds her security in her relationship with Jesus Christ. She is not quick to flaunt what she knows, or what she looks like. She is not impulsive, or loud. She does not talk about everything that comes to mind. She is happy to be silent and hidden. Rather than a pig with a ring of gold through its snout, she is a like a rare gem that is quarried from deep within the earth, hidden for a time until discovered by those who recognize her true beauty and value.[xxii]

Amy Miller - Share Faith

We have a generation of young women who have never been introduced or discipled in the area of discretion. Women who are mature in Christ are responsible to pass along the godly wisdom that will help the next generation avoid foolish and unwise choices and preserve their witness for Christ.

Let's Talk…

1. Look up the word "flaunt" in a dictionary and write out the definition. Give some examples from the culture that reflect this idea of women "flaunting" themselves.

2. Oxford's Dictionary voted "SELFIE" as the 2013 Word of the Year. A "selfie" is defined as a photograph that one has taken of oneself, typically one taken with a smartphone or webcam and uploaded to a social media website.

   Many of us have posted a "selfie" to social media; some of us have posted *several*. Why do you think women purposefully post pictures of themselves in order to gain flattering comments?

3. The godly characteristics of a woman are ridiculed in today's culture. Even Christian women believe that the Bible is not relevant when it comes to topics like discretion and modesty. What does Isaiah warn us about in Isaiah 5:20?

4. Give some examples where the culture has defined ungodly behavior of women "good."

5. Read Proverbs 7:1-27. In what ways do we see women in the world walking in the path of the women described in this passage?

6. List the "indiscreet" ways of the woman described in Proverbs 7:1-27.

   What is her ultimate end?

7. Are you a girl gone wild, or a girl gone wise? That is the question Mary Kassian asks in her book, *"Girls Gone Wise in a World gone Wild."*[xxiii] The world dares women to live wildly, with reckless abandon, leaving all wisdom behind. Romans 13:13 in the RSV speaks to the sin of licentiousness. "Aselgia" is the Greek word for licentiousness and is defined as unbridled lust, excess, lasciviousness, wantonness, outrageousness, shamelessness, insolence.

   Describe some of the reckless behavior of women you see promoted in the media today. Consider social media, the internet, movies, television shows, books and magazines. What are some of the consequences to this way of living?

8. Read Proverbs 5:5-6. "Indiscretion" can involve a pattern of making bad choices leading a woman to become "unstable". What are some practical ways a woman can begin to develop wisdom and begin to make responsible choices? Use Scripture to support your answer.

9. Write out 1 Timothy 2:9-10 using your own words.

10. Share some practical ways women can walk in the truth of 1 Timothy 2:9-10 both in modesty and professing godliness with good works.

MEEKNESS OR WEAKNESS

Do not let your adornment be merely outward—arranging the hair, wearing gold, or putting on fine apparel — rather let it be the hidden person of the heart, with the incorruptible beauty of a gentle and quiet spirit, which is very precious in the sight of God.

1 Peter 3:3-4

The Conversation

One of my great childhood memories was the Christmas I received "Chatty Cathy". She was a doll manufactured by Mattel in 1959 that spoke eleven different phrases. Seven more sentences were added to her vocabulary in 1963 and she became the 2nd most popular doll of the 1960's after Barbie. After all from the time we are little girls, we love to chat!!!

Perhaps that is why God teaches us in His Word that a gentle and quiet spirit is precious to Him, because the natural woman loves to talk. How difficult it is for me and you to stay quiet when we absolutely believe that what we have to say must be heard!

It has been said that women speak 20,000 words a day compared to the 7,000 men utter. There is much debate about the truth of this statement, but I find it more than revealing that 1 Peter 3:3-4 is not written to men. For this reason we understand that these verses are a foundational piece of biblical womanhood that we should desire to seek to develop in our walks with Christ.

The word "precious" used here means "costly", "of great price", "excellent" and "of surpassing value". In other words this gentle and quiet spirit is going to go a long way in the life of a woman to bring God glory. It is the same word used to describe the spikenard that Mary of Bethany used to pour on Jesus' head.

A "gentle and quiet" spirit is often looked upon by women as less than desirable until she comes to embrace its deeper implication. The word "meekness", used in other translations, describes a soothing medicine, a gentle breeze, or a colt that has been broken and domesticated. Tied up in the word meek is the concept of power under control, the idea of being submissive to Someone greater than ourselves. The idea of power under control is best translated by the English word "gentleness." It is anything but "weakness."

Scripture teaches us that "...Out of the abundance of the heart the mouth speaks." (Luke 6:45). This character that is so precious to God is developed when we sit at His feet and care for the inner woman more than the outer woman. We allow His Word and Holy Spirit to keep our hearts soft and sensitive to those around us. And of the utmost importance, when the need to be "Chatty Cathy" takes over, let us consider and carefully weigh our words and remember a gentle and quiet spirit is precious in the sight of God.

Let's Talk...

1. Matthew Henry's commentary on 1 Peter 3:3-4 is helpful as we seek to reflect on the idea of a gentle and quiet spirit:

    "It is 'in the sight of God of great price.' It is really a precious grace, for it is so in the sight of God ... Herein we should every one labor and this we should be ambitious of, as of the greatest honor ... it is a thing attainable through the Mediator from whom we have received instruction how to walk so as to please him. We must walk with meekness and quietness of spirit, for this is 'in the sight of God of great price.' Therefore this mark of honor is, in a special measure, put upon the grace of meekness, because it is commonly despised and looked upon with contempt by the children of the world ... meekness and quietness of spirit is a very excellent grace which we should every one of us put on and be adorned with." [xxiv]

    Why do you think God deems it precious when a woman walks with meekness and a quietness of spirit? Why do you think He addressed this command to women specifically?

2. Look up the following verses and in two or three sentences form your own definition of meekness.

    - 2 Corinthians 10:1

    - Colossians 3:12

    - James 1:21

    - James 3:13

    - 1 Peter 3:15

3. It is helpful in understanding meekness to consider its' opposite. Read 3 John 1: 9-10 and describe the character of Diotrophes.

4. The culture would ascribe much to Diotrophes, claiming he was aggressive, self-assertive and ambitious. The world would maintain that his qualities are necessary to be successful and to "get ahead." How do these qualities stand in direct opposition to "meekness"?

5. What does it mean "to love the preeminence"?

6. How is the culture promoting the "preeminence" of women?

7. Why is it easy for women to adopt some of the culture's "preeminence" thinking? Explain your answer.

8. "Preeminence" is responsible for many an argument. It's interesting to note that God highlights in Scripture that "contention" can be a real problem for women. Record what you discover.

    - Proverbs 21:9

    - Proverbs 21:19

    - Proverbs 25:24

    - Proverbs 27:15

9. Sometimes "no response" is better than speaking. Do you struggle with keeping silent? Why or why not?

10. Using the illustrations below, give some examples of practical ways "meekness" can be worked out in your life. Consider in your examples your words as well as your actions.

    - A soothing medicine that brings healing and comfort

    - A gentle breeze that brings relief and refreshment

    - A broken colt who is now useful and not destructive

WOMEN OR MEN?

And I do not permit a woman to teach or to have authority over a man, but to be in silence.

1 Timothy 2:12

The Conversation

This week's conversation may be the most "controversial." Along with feminism and feminist liberation theology, came the opening of the pulpit to women pastors. This ignited a debate (which we discussed in an earlier conversation) between those who believed that anyone, male or female, should be allowed to assume any position in the Church (egalitarians) and those who believed that while men and women are equal, God has assigned them different roles (complementarians).

While there are those on both sides of the debate, it is what the Bible teaches, that we are after. We will discover in our time of study that 1 Timothy 2:12 clearly teaches women are not to serve in any role which involves the authoritative spiritual teaching of men. Instead of focusing on a role God has clearly deemed for men, a woman can enjoy and celebrate the multitudes of ways God calls and gifts her to serve. Eve had her choice of every tree in the garden, yet she believed God was holding out on her when He commanded, "…Of every tree of the garden you may freely eat; but of the tree of the knowledge of good and evil you shall not eat, for in the day that you eat of it you shall surely die (Genesis 2:16).

We see women living extraordinary lives throughout the Bible. We witness God placing them in critical roles that changed the course of history. We watch them minister side by side with Jesus. In the New Testament Epistles, they share an active and prominent role in proclaiming the gospel, teaching women and children. When serving in the roles God has uniquely designed for women, they flourish.

Yet, the desire for a woman to usurp a man's role, is far more widespread than the "pastor" issue. The neutrality of gender roles are a hot topic in the world today. The lies permeating the culture are a clear advancing of the enemy's plan to destroy the God-given distinction between men and women that is meant to bring glory to God.

Pay close attention to what you study this week. Wrestle with the texts and ask the hard questions. Make sure that nowhere in your thinking are you entertaining thoughts that somehow God is biased.

Let's Talk...

It is key as we cover this area, that we are clear on what the Scriptures teach:

1. Compare 1st Timothy 3:2 and Titus 1:5-6 as it relates to the overseer/bishop of the church. The phrase "husband of one wife" is in the Greek "mias guniakso aner" which is literally, "man of one woman." This means that the elder has to be a male because a woman cannot be a "man of one woman." Therefore, a woman is not to be an elder or a pastor in the church. It is also interesting to note that in the mention of over 700 priests in the Old Testament, every single one was a male.

   Why do you think there is so much controversy wrapped around women elders and pastors when it is clear the Bible teaches these roles are for men?

2. Many in the church today teach that certain portions of Scripture are not relevant to the times in which we live. Do you agree? Why or why not? Support either answer with Scripture.

3. Louisiana State University's student newspaper, The Daily Reveille, published an online article on September 8, 2014 titled, *Genderless Fashion Emerges*. Read the following excerpt:

   "Everyone" fashion breaks away from "men's" and "women's" clothing to create its own identity. To put it simply, gender roles and rules are changing. We can't put everyone into little boxes labeled "male" or "female." We also can't expect that because someone is a woman she'll want either women's clothing, or women's clothing marketed as "The Boyfriend" fit. The same applies to men. Everything I've previously described would be considered unisex, or clothing that can fit both genders. But the fashion industry is now breaking down all gender-related titles and creating a new title: Everyone. "Everyone" is a genderless section of clothing. Whatever the consumer considers themselves, they can find something in the "everyone" section.[xxv] – Meg Ryan

   - Comment on how the culture is promoting a lack of distinction between men and women. Cite some other examples.

4. It is no longer sufficient to offer only two boxes to check on college applications that indicate gender, male or female. Consider Smith College for Women in North Hampton, Massachutes. The following information is taken directly from their website.[xxvi]

> *Gender Identity and Gender Expression at Smith*
>
> Transgender students looking at colleges often have specific questions about gender diversity on campus. There are special considerations for transgender students in applying to a women's college.
>
> **Does Smith have transgender students?**
> Like nearly every college, university and school today, Smith College has a diverse and dynamic student body that includes individuals who identify as transgender. Students at Smith, whatever their gender identity or gender expression are diverse, accomplished, and various in their views.
>
> **Is Smith still a women's college?**
> Absolutely. In its mission and legal status, Smith is a women's college. And, like other women's colleges, Smith is a place where students are able to explore who they are in an open and respectful environment.
>
> **How does Smith decide who is a woman?**
> It doesn't. With regard to admission, Smith relies upon the information provided by each student applicant. In other contexts, different definitions and requirements may apply. For example, the definition of a woman for NCAA competition may differ from the definition of a woman for purposes of admission to Smith or other single-sex colleges.

- The culture now defines gender. How does this self-definition oppose the teaching of God and Scripture? Use Scripture to support your answer.

5. Read Romans 1:18-32. What are the logical conclusions of a "transgender" thinking? In light of those conclusions, why is it so important that we cling to biblical truth?

6. Many women in and out of the church struggle with the sin of homosexuality. Read the following letter from a sister in Christ that was written to the Gospel Coalition and reprinted by Hunter Baker on their website on January 13, 2013.[xxvii]

> To the churches concerning homosexuals and lesbians from a sister in Christ
>
> Many of you believe that we do not exist within your walls, your schools, your neighborhoods. You believe that we are few and easily recognized. I tell you we are many. We are your teachers, doctors, accountants, high school athletes. We are all colors, shapes, sizes. We are single, married, mothers, fathers. We are your sons, your daughters, your nieces, your nephews, your grandchildren. We are in your Sunday school classes, pews, choirs, and pulpits. You choose not to see us out of ignorance or because it might upset your congregation. We ARE your congregation. We enter your doors weekly seeking guidance and some glimmer of hope that we can change. Like you, we have invited Jesus into our hearts. Like you, we want to be all that Christ wants us to be. Like you, we pray daily for guidance. Like you, we often fail.
>
> When the word "homosexual" is mentioned in the church, we hold our breaths and sit in fear. Most often this word is followed with condemnation, laughter, hatred, or jokes. Rarely do we hear any words of hope. At least we recognize our sin. Does the church as a whole see theirs? Do you see the sin of pride, that you are better than or more acceptable to Jesus than we are? Have you been Christ-like in your relationships with us? Would you meet us at the well, or restaurant, for a cup of water, or coffee? Would you touch us even if we showed signs of leprosy, or aids? Would you call us down from our trees, as Christ did Zacchaeus, and invite yourself to be our guest? Would you allow us to sit at your table and break bread? Can you love us unconditionally and support us as Christ works in our lives, as He works in yours, to help us all to overcome?
>
> To those of you who would change the church to accept the gay community and its lifestyle: you give us no hope at all. To those of us who know God's word and will not dilute it to fit our desires, we ask you to read John's letter to the church in Pergamum. "I have a few things against you: You have people there who hold to the teaching of Balaam, who taught Balak to entice the Israelites to sin by eating food sacrificed to idols and by committing sexual immorality. Likewise, you also have those who hold to the teaching of the Nicolaitans. Repent therefore!" You are willing to compromise the word of God to be politically correct. We are not deceived. If we accept your willingness to compromise, then we must also compromise. We must therefore accept your lying, your adultery, your lust, your idolatry, your addictions, YOUR sins. "He who has an ear, let him hear what the Spirit says to the churches."
>
> We do not ask for your acceptance of our sins any more than we accept yours. We simply ask for the same support, love, guidance, and most of all hope that is given to the rest of your congregation. We are your brothers and sisters in Christ. We are not what we shall be, but thank God, we are not what we were. Let us work together to see that we all arrive safely home.

7. How does the author of this letter address the sin of homosexuality in the church? Do you agree or disagree? Explain your answer in depth.

8. Is homosexuality an orientation God intended for some people, or is it a perversion of normal sexuality? Support your answer with Scripture.

9. The presence of abuse is a recurring theme in the early lives of many homosexual strugglers. In one study, 91% of lesbian women reported childhood and adolescent abuse, 2/3 of them victims of sexual abuse.[xxviii]

   How should this statistic impact our ministry to women who struggle with lesbianism?

10. Identify an areas of faulty thinking this lesson may have corrected for you.

RETIRE OR INSPIRE?

The older women likewise, that they be reverent in behavior, not slanderers, not given to much wine, teachers of good things— that they admonish the young women to love their husbands, to love their children, to be discreet, chaste, homemakers, good, obedient to their own husbands, that the word of God may not be blasphemed.

Titus 2:3-5

The Conversation

In my eleven years of ministry to women, I have had the opportunity and great blessing to encourage, mentor and equip women, both young and old. A few years ago, it came as quite a surprise to me to discover that the "older" women were disappearing from the landscape of the church. Many mentoring ministries died, not for a lack of younger women desiring that kind of relationship, but for the lack of older women available to meet the need.

Digging deeper into the absence of the "senior" woman, I found that there were many attitudes at play. The first was *"I've done my time, it's time for me to retire."* The second attitude was, *"I have nothing to offer."* And third was, *"My church has placed me on the shelf."* Whatever one of these three mindsets an older woman may adopt, she must understand that all three are unbiblical.

The truth is that a woman's later years are to be her most fruitful. This is the season where she fully blooms, embracing every aspect of her womanhood. She is not to "retire" but to "inspire" the next generation. Her walk with God, her life experiences and godly wisdom are valuable treasure to the younger woman who seeks to fulfill her God-given purpose. As she invests in the next generation, her heart stays passionate and alive. She has the blessing of watching the younger woman accomplish greater things than she was able to. This time is truly the "peak" of her life.

This final conversation is important for every woman, both young and old. As you study through the pages of Scripture, you will see the beautiful path that God has paved for you to travel on through the years. If you join Him on that path, your life will be filled with fruit that is sweet and fragrant, with loving relationships and an eternal legacy that pleases and honors God.

Let's Talk...

1. Read 1 Timothy 5:3-16. In these verses, the church is instructed to honor "widows" who are really "widows." Describe the characteristics of a "true" widow.

2. You might be wondering what Paul meant when he said that a widow who lives "in pleasure is dead while she lives."

    "The pleasure Paul was speaking against is voluptuousness. The word "voluptuous" means "devoted to or indulging in sensual pleasures" (American Heritage Dictionary). Paul was saying that a widow who is not serving God and others but lives only for self is not really living. The word "dead" is being used in an allegorical sense.[xxix]

    Andrew Wommack

    What does this verse teach us about "retirement" for a woman in her later years?

3. In the early church, there was a list of widows. Their godly lifestyles were responsible for their names being on the list. Some who didn't have families were cared for by the church and some were not, but they were official servants of the church – they were there to serve God's church. If you go back into the history of the church they had fairly defined responsibility. They would visit the church's younger women (that was a priority obviously drawn from Titus 2) and visit these younger women to teach them, to instruct them, to help them in daily tasks, to show them things about being wise, and about being mothers, and about being homemakers. They had an ongoing responsibility to be available to those women in the church who needed their help. These women who were 60 and over had tremendous influence and were key to a powerful witness in their communities.

    Do you see an influence of older women in your church and community? Explain your answer.

4. One of the ministries in which the widows served was quite unique. They would go through the city streets and the market place, on a daily basis, to pick up the babies that had been left there. Ancient times also experienced a "Woman's Liberation Movement," especially in the time of Paul. Women didn't have the means of abortion that people have today, because they didn't have the medical advancement, so they gave birth to their baby and just left it in the marketplace.

   Male children would be picked up and trained to be gladiators; female children would be picked up and trained to be prostitutes. In order to save these little lives, Christian widows, those who were on the church list, would comb the marketplace and the public places of the city daily, and they would scoop up the little lives and put them in Christian families so that they could be raised to be Christian young people.

   - What are some ways today that older women can serve in a similar manner?

5. The older woman is to be a teacher of "good things." Literally the Greek word here could be translated "teachers of what is good." "Good" being a word that means noble, excellent, lofty. This word is to the idea of the very life the women live, becoming a model or a pattern of goodness, responsible to become teachers of the next generation. They do that by mentoring, by discipling, by modeling, by setting the example of godly living with regard to marriage and the family and the home.

   - In this season of your life, identify the ways you are being a teacher of good things.

6. The word "blasphemed" is a transliteration of the Greek word *blasphemeo*. The word means "to vilify, to speak impiously, or to speak evil of." Give some examples of how women might blaspheme the Word of God in light of the passage's context?

7. If you are a younger married woman, we learn a lot about your focus and purpose for this season of your lives in Titus 2:4-5. Summarize that focus and purpose.

8. Read 1 Corinthians 7:32-35. In contrast to the married woman, what is the priority of women who are single? Why is "marriage" a distraction according to Paul?

9. If you are a single woman, do you see your "singleness" as a gift from God? Why or why not?

10. Take a moment to consider how Scripture has opened up your eyes to the truth of what it means to be a woman. How will you incorporate these truths in your life and how will you use them to evangelize and disciple other women?

ENDNOTES

[i] Mary A. Kassian. The Feminist Mistake. Crossway Books. (Wheaton, Illinois 2007).

[ii] Wayne Grudem. Biblical Foundations for Manhood and Womanhood. Crossway Books (Wheaton, Illinois 2002).

[iii] Caleb Colley, Ph.D. God is No Respecter of Persons. Apologetics Press (2004) http://www.apologeticspress.org/APContent.aspx?category=111&article=1440

[iv] S. Michael Houdmann. What does the Bible say about Feminism? http://www.gotquestions.org/feminism-Christian-feminist.html

[v] Elisabeth Elliot. Portraying Christian Femininity. http://cbmw.org/uncategorized/portraying-christian-femininity/

[vi] Nancy Leigh DeMoss. Becoming God's True Woman. Crossway Books. (Wheaton, Illinois 2008).

[vii] Ibid, Kassian.

[viii] Ibid, Houdmann

[ix] W. A. Criswell. Hebrew Word Study. http://www.preceptaustin.org/hebrew_word_study_on_help.htm

[x] Donald Guthrie. The New Bible Commentary. Eerdmans Publishing (Grand Rapids, Michigan 1970).

[xi] John Piper. The Ultimate Meaning of True Womanhood. http://www.desiringgod.org/conference-messages/the-ultimate-meaning-of-true-womanhood

[xii] Donald Davidson. Mothers in the Bible. Zondervan (1958).

[xiii] Sally Clarkson. The Mission of Motherhood. Waterbrook Press (Colorado Springs, Colorado 2003)

[xiv] Charles Spurgeon. The Tender Comfort of God's Love. (Sermon No. 3189, 1910) http://www.ccel.org/ccel/spurgeon/sermons56.xii.html

[xv] Beth Moore. Spiritual Mothering. (2000) http://www.lifeway.com/Article/Spiritual-mothering

[xvi] Tammy Maltby. Lifegiving. Moody Publishers (Chicago, Illinois 2002)

[xvii] Burt Bacharach and Hal David. A House is Not a Home. (Scepter Label Manhattan, New York 1964)

[xviii] Ibid, Nancy Leigh DeMoss

[xix] J.D. Davis. Lydia: A Model of Service and Hospitality Acts 16 (May 2006) http://www.lifeway.com/Article/sermon-lydia-model-service-hospitality-acts-16

[xx] Max Lucado. Outlive Your Life. Max Lucado (2010).

[xxi] Ibid, Tammy Maltby

[xxii] Amy Miller. What is a Godly Woman: The Virtue of Discretion. http://www.sharefaith.com/guide/christian-principles/virtues-of-godly-women/virute-of-discretion.html

[xxiii] Mary Kassian. Girls Gone Wise. Moody Publishers (Chicago, Illinois 2010).

[xxiv] Matthew Henry. The Characteristics of a Meek and Quiet Spirit. https://www.reviveourhearts.com/articles/characteristics-meek-and-quiet-spirit/

[xxv] Meg Ryan. Genderless Fashion Trend Emerges. (September 2014). http://www.lsureveille.com/entertainment/genderless-fashion-trend-emerges/article_ae00f896-33d5-11e4-a98e-0017a43b2370.html

[xxvi] Smith College. Gender Identity and Expression. http://www.smith.edu/diversity/gender.php

[xxvii] Hunter Baker. An Open Letter to the Church from a Lesbian. http://www.thegospelcoalition.org/blogs/justintaylor/2013/03/21/an-open-letter-to-the-church-from-a-lesbian/

[xxviii] Anne Paulk, Restoring Sexual Identity, Harvest House (Eugene, Oregon, 2003).

[xxix] Andrew Wommack. 1 Timothy 5:6. http://www.awmi.net/bible/1ti_05_06

Made in the USA
Charleston, SC
12 March 2016